The Great Marathon Football Match

Janet and Allan Ahlberg

Collins

The Brick Street Boys all play football
for the school team.
The team's mascot is a dog called Scruffy.

Sometimes he goes to school as well.

Scruffy likes school.
He likes the lessons.
He likes playtimes.
But most of all he likes Mr Mott
and playing football with the Brick Street Boys.

Mr Mott is the football teacher.
One day when the boys were getting ready for
a practice match he said,
"I think we need some new shirts."
"And shorts!" said Sam.
"And socks!" said Fred.
"No," said Ambrose, "we could mend them."
"Easy," said Stanley.
"Let's try it," said Bruce. So they did.

When they had finished Mr Mott said,
"I still think we need some new shirts."
"You're right," said Ambrose.
"We do," said Fred.
"Definitely," said Sam.
"Wuff," said Scruffy.

Then some of the boys began to say what colours the new kit should be. Some of them began to daydream what it would be like.

All of them wanted to go out and buy it
straight away.

So they did.

All the boys worked very hard.
They got their mothers to sort out old clothes
and make cakes for the cake stall.

They got their fathers to carry the jumble to
the school.

Their sisters helped to run the stalls.

When the Jumble Sale was over the boys
counted the money.
"I make it £7.56," said Sam.
"I make it £13.23½," said Fred.
"I don't make it anything at all," said Stanley.
"I can't count." Mr Mott made it £8.26, three
old pennies and a button. And it was.

All the boys were happy.
"£8.26!" they said, "and three old pennies,
and a button!"
"It's not enough," said Mr Mott, "we need
more." So the boys began to think how they
could get some more money. All except Trevor
who began to think how soon he would get his tea.

"I could ask the infants for some," said Fred.
"I don't think so," said Mr Mott.

"I could do jobs for people," said Sam.
"And me!" said Eric.
"And me!" said Ambrose.
"And me, and me!" said everybody.
So they did.

Scruffy fetched Mr Green's newspaper. Stanley and Fred tidied up Mrs Green's garden.

Bruce told fortunes.

Sam took dogs for a walk. Trevor and Ambrose
and Eric and Eric's little sisters cleaned windows.

When all the jobs were finished the boys had collected another £4.97.

"Altogether that makes £12.63," said Sam.

"Altogether that makes £17.82," said Fred.

"Altogether that makes . . . more than we had before," said Stanley.

Mr Mott said altogether it made £13.23.

And it did. All the boys were very happy.

"£13.23!" they said, "we'll soon be rich. We'll soon be millionaires!"

"It's not enough," said Mr Mott, "we still need more."

So the boys began again to think how to get
some more money. All except Bruce who was
thinking about what he was going to be when
he grew up.

"Let's have a marathon football match," said Eric.
"Yes," said Ambrose, "and get money for
every hour we play."
"We could have Sam's team against Fred's
team," said Stanley.
"Great!" said Sam.
"We'll flatten you!" said Fred.
So on Saturday morning "The Great Brick
Street School Marathon Football Match" began.

By dinner time Fred's team was winning 18–13.

By tea time Sam's team was winning 56–49.

By supper time the score was 98–98.

By bedtime nobody knew what the score was
but Stanley said it was quite a lot.

On Sunday everybody was very tired.
Sam stayed in bed till three o'clock.
Fred stayed in bed till four o'clock.
Eric didn't get up till it was time to go to bed.
Mr Mott didn't get up at all.

The next day the boys worked out how much
money they had made.
"All of us together were sponsored at £1.83 an
hour," said Sam. "and we played for nine
hours. So that makes . . ." He began working
it out. Fred began working it out too.
Stanley didn't bother working it out.

"It makes enough," said Mr Mott, "we can buy the shirts."

"And shorts!" said Sam.

"And socks!" said Fred.

"And have a party as well," said Mr Mott.

"Hurray!" said Sam and Fred.

"Hurray!" said Ambrose and Stanley and Eric.

"Hurray, hurray!" said everybody, "We can have a party!"

So they did.

After the party was over Mr Mott took a
photograph of the boys in their new kit.

The sun shone down.
"Lovely weather," said Sam's mum.
"Beautiful," said Fred's dad, "soon be time
for cricket."

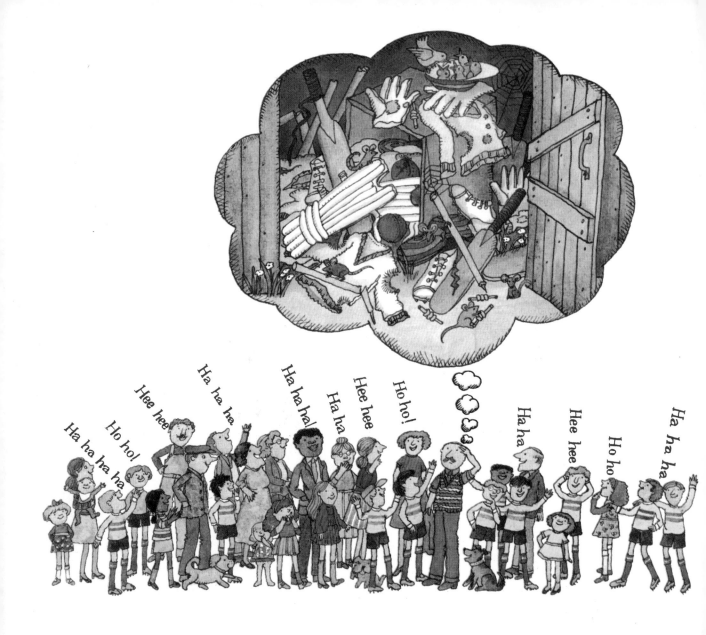

"Yes," said Mr Mott, "I've been thinking about cricket."
Then everybody started to laugh.

Other books about the Brick Street Boys:

Here are the Brick Street Boys
A Place to Play
Sam the Referee
Fred's Dream

First published 1976
This edition 1986
© Janet and Allan Ahlberg 1976

ISBN 0 00 138014-1

Printed in Italy by New Interlitho, Milan